CINDY STEWART

NEW MOVES
OF GOD

NEW MOVES OF GOD

Copyright © 2022 Cynthia Stewart

TABLE OF CONTENTS

WELCOME TO THE *NEW MOVES OF GOD!*

God has been highlighting what He is doing in this season. One day He gave me the assignment to write this book highlighting some of His new moves.

God is positioning us for one of the most significant invasions of world culture in Kingdom history. God is releasing new anointings and new assignments that will far surpass our wildest imaginations.

This book will open your spiritual eyes to see what God is doing. I have shared the revelation that God has shown me. I have included activations, impartation, and testimonies with each chapter to empower you to step into position.

I pray for the Lord to open your eyes to identify your role in His new moves. The Lord will open doors, extend favor to position you, and equip you for this new season. In Jesus's Name, Amen.

"Moreover the word of the LORD came to me, saying, 'Jeremiah, what do you see?' And I said, 'I see a branch of an almond tree.' Then the LORD said to me, 'You have seen well, for I am ready to perform My word.' —Jeremiah 1:11-12 (NKJV)

Thank you for jumping in with me!

—Cindy Stewart

Chapter One

NEW MOVES

Are you ready for God's new move?

I was sitting in my comfy chair reading Proverbs 4:25-26 in the *Passion Translation*.

"Set your gaze on the path before you.
  With fixed purpose, looking straight ahead,
  ignore life's distractions.
  Watch where you're going!
  Stick to the path of truth,
  and the road will be safe and smooth before you."

Immediately, in a vision, I saw a narrow dirt path lined with lush greenery.

I asked Jesus, "What are You showing me?"

He replied, "You can only see a short distance ahead. The path is narrow but clear. Follow My path I have laid out for you."

There are new paths He is leading us on.

There are new ways He wants us to do things.

To travel the new path, we must follow the lead of the Spirit, which brings us into God's new way.

God's new path will take us beyond what is normal and what we believe is possible, leading us to the impossible made possible.

I have found that this new way of doing things is critical for us to grab a hold of and understand. We must follow the new way the Spirit leads us to step into God's way in everything we do in our life. God has a new way for us to step into in everything we do.

I am particularly excited about this because God has something for us that we are intellectually unaware of but spiritually prepared to do.

Our minds cannot conceive what God has planned for us. However, God has prepared our spirits to release the plan He has put in us.

Isaiah 43:18-19 says,

> "Do not remember the former things nor consider the things of old. Behold, I will do a new thing. Now it shall spring forth. Shall you not know it? I will even make a road in the wilderness and rivers in the desert." (NKJV)

God is moving us out of the old ways, away from the former things. Out of the old into the new.

We go through moves with God. Some of them last fifty years while others last ten years. Whatever length the move is, we are all in the same flow; we're in the same process, and it works for that season of time. It is time to embrace the new move of God by learning new ways.

An example of the new "move" or "God's new way" can be found in the healing movement. Oral Roberts' anointing was to create a point of contact by laying hands on every person to release healing. In the years to follow, Kathryn Kuhlman was anointed to just release the healing power of God through her spoken words. It was no longer necessary to lay hands on every person.

Do you recognize the shift from the familiar way to God's new way?

God wants to transition us from what has worked in the past to what will work in this new season. By following the new way, we will move to a greater level for a more significant expansion of what He has for us.

This transition period can be challenging because our brain develops neural pathways, repeated thoughts and actions, that wire our mind to respond with little thought. In other words, when we drive the same way home every day, our route develops a neural pathway like an auto-pilot. So, when we try new things, we build new neural pathways or turn the auto-pilot off.

We know when God shows us a new way we have to build this new way into our lives because when we just see or do it once, the new way can be lost.

When we go a new way, we must incorporate the new system so we can follow the new way.

We do this by leaning into the Word of God and understanding what He has for this season.

Many of us have read Isaiah 43:18-19, many times. Perhaps you have heard it prophesied many times, and in different seasons, God is doing something new.

When we hear a Scripture that has brought us breakthrough in the past, we often put it in the past, not realizing how God wants to activate it for the future. And sometimes we discount those Scriptures because of it.

For instance...

Twenty years ago, when I heard Isaiah 43:18-19, God was taking me to new levels of encounters with Him. So, when I hear that Scripture now, I recall the breakthrough of the past. But, what God is trying to show me through this Scripture is that the breakthrough it brought in the past is now the new move for the future.

We need to acknowledge it as a testimony of what God has done, and move forward in the new thing God wants to do for us.

LET ME BRAG ON JESUS

(That is what we call testimony in our church.)

God decided to change up my morning time with Him. He said, "I want you to pray in the Spirit, then take Communion, and then read the Word." The first day I read the Word, prayed in the Spirit, and took Communion.

The next day God says, "No! I want you to pray in the Spirit first." So, I prayed in the Spirit, took Communion, and read the Word.

The Word became fat and juicy. New revelation dripped from each Word, because I followed "God's new way."

I had not done my devotions in that order before.

The difference was I prepared my mind to be transformed by the building up of my spirit. My routine was to read the Word, pray in the Spirit, and then take Communion, but God wanted to do something new.

Why don't you try this? Set your timer for a few minutes to pray in the Spirit, then take Communion, and read the Word. You will see a new illumination of the Word of God.

God wants to release His "new move" to you this season.

BECOMING A PART OF THE NEW MOVE

Many places in the Word give solutions for today's issues.

When you need a solution, you can find Scripture that answers the problem.

You may need a solution for lack in your finances, your physical body, or infertility, no matter what.

We don't have to live in barrenness (lack) because we have the Word of the Lord that will bring us solutions to fullness.

The Word of God will activate the breaking off of barrenness, unfruitfulness, infertility, bleakness and unproductiveness. And the Word of God will give you His supernatural solution to prosperity in the area needed.

You just need to know what you are looking at.

Allow me to show you revelation of the "new way" God has shown me.

For every issue you have, God has a solution.

And I am going to teach you how to recognize your solution in God's Word.

First and foremost, you must know the character and nature of God, and that is only acquired by knowing His Word and spending time with Him.

Knowing His word brings you into a deep personal

relationship with Him. You cannot have a relationship without knowing the Word, since He is the Word.

Your solution is in the Word, and God is inviting you to partner with Him to find your solution. Not as a last resort, but to seek Him first.

In reading God's Word, it is essential to understand His Word is not always literal. The Bible is written with various figures of speech.

Symbolism (representative) and metaphorical (designates one thing, is used to designate another) and imagery (a representation of the form of a person or object) are only three.

We often read Scripture, but we don't have the connection to the symbols and metaphors for God's Word. By identifying these we can discern the interpretation to help us find the resolution.

For instance, today's issues of fruitlessness, lack, and infertility have solutions in God's Word.

The Bible uses the word "barrenness" to describe all three, but without knowing this, we would read right over these passages and miss our solution.

Together, let's look at these examples in Scripture.

1. Unfruitfulness – Barrenness in the Land

In 2 Kings, Elisha succeeded Elijah as the prophet. He was faced with many situations that needed supernatural solutions.

"Then the men of the city said to Elisha, 'Please notice, the situation of the city is pleasant, as my Lord sees; but the water is bad, and the ground is *barren*.' And he said, 'Bring me a new bowl, and put salt in it.' So, they brought it to him. Then he went out to the source of the water, and cast in the salt there, and said, 'Thus says, the Lord: "I have healed this water; from it, there shall be no more death or barrenness."' So, the water remains healed to this day, according to the Word of Elisha, which he spoke.' —2 Kings 2:19-22 (NKJV)

The issue is the barrenness or unfruitfulness of the land from the bad water.

Like bad water yielding to unfruitfulness, we cannot produce when our source is bad. Our barrenness can be a product of bitterness, offense, or unforgiveness (not exclusive).

Just as Elisha used the salt to heal the water so the land could produce, God wants to reveal to you the source of unfruitfulness in your life.

Notice that Elisha works out of a "Oneness" of God. Elisha had experience with the character and nature of God, knowing it was in God's nature for the water to be healed. He then was able to make the land fruitful again by healing the water.

God never gave Elisha the step-by step instructions; God simply backed Elisha's actions out of their relationship – Oneness.

Elisha broke the barrenness in a way that had never been done before. It wasn't written in a manual. He simply took a bowl, added salt, and threw it into the water. When the salt hit the water, the water was immediately healed. With the water healed, the ground became fruitful again.

Elisha brought breakthrough for their "barrenness" by following a new way of God.

It was something outside the realm of the ordinary. This is what we must learn to do - look outside of the realm of the normal to the spiritual realm.

When we learn to do this, we will begin to see the solutions of God.

LET ME BRAG ON JESUS

We knew someone one who struggled with not knowing their identity in Christ, and it manifested as unworthiness and self-hatred. All of these things were feeding their unfruitfulness to the point of afflicting self-harm.

In working with God, they discovered the multiple sources of the "bad water" and began to seek God for the "new way." God removed unworthiness and self-hatred, replacing it with the truth of their identity. He healed the pain, which stopped the self-harm.

They grew stronger in their anointing of reaching others who also struggle with these areas. They have led many to Christ.

Now, having completed Bible College, they are moving into a new position with a global ministry that houses others in crisis.

2. Lack - Barrenness in Our Finances

"But you shall remember [with profound respect] the LORD your God, for it is He who is giving you power to make wealth..." —Deuteronomy 8:18 (AMP)

We know that sometimes financial prosperity comes out of the small things that we already have and is added to by others.

As believers, we often hesitate to ask for help because we think we should be self-sufficient in getting out of a lack.

Jesus wants us to prosper and He will use the willingness of others to aid us in creating wealth.

2 Kings 4 tells of a widow who cannot provide for her family; she has a lack.

In the community of prophets there was a widow who sought Elisha for help. Her husband is dead, she owes the creditors, and now they are threatening to take her sons. She doesn't have any money to provide for her family.

"So, Elisha said to her, 'What shall I do for you? Tell me, what do you have in the house?' And she said, 'Your maidservant has nothing in the house but a jar of oil.' Then he said, 'Go borrow vessels from everywhere, from all your neighbors-empty vessels; do not gather just a few. And when you have come in, you shall shut the door behind you and your sons; then pour it into all those vessels, and set aside the full ones.' So, she went from him and shut the door behind her and her sons, who brought the vessels to her; and she poured it out.

Now it came to pass, when the vessels were full, that she said to her son, 'Bring me another vessel.' And he said to her, 'There is not another vessel.' So the oil ceased. Then she came and told the man of God. And he said, 'Go sell the oil and pay your debt; and you and your sons live on the rest.'"—2 Kings 4:2-7 (NKJV)

Instead of her sons being carted off as slaves and the widow ending up in the street, she became a model citizen in her neighborhood by paying back her debts, and her sons became viable prospects for marriage, which blessed the community.

End result – the widow and her family prospered.

Why did she prosper?

Because she was obedient.

The widow and her sons took every vessel and filled it; filled the next one, and the next one, and the next one, until there were no more empty vessels. They didn't run out of oil, and nor did they have vessels leftover.

When you receive what God has for you, then you won't have a need anymore. Since He is a God of perfect funding – supplying what you need.

What is your small beginning?

You can take your small beginning and put God's anointing on it by being obedient to His instruction, and trusting God for the outcome. Then declare it to be multiplied.

We stand on the fact that God is able to do immeasurably more than we could ever dream or imagine, in every situation, in every occurrence, in every moment of every day.

LET ME BRAG ON JESUS

Each day I post a "Positive Word" on social media (@ cindystewartlive).

Here is one of my recent posts:

"Today, I will look for ways to pay off my debt."

I received this testimony in response.

I'm contending for debt-free strategies. The Hospital just forgave my recent Emergency Room bill that was $5,000!

A week or so later, I received another testimony from the same person:

Good morning, Cindy:

God just wiped out ANOTHER $5,000 of my debt! That's $10,000 in the month of July! I'm contending to be debt-free by Nov 5, and God's doing it! The timing is perfect!!

$10,000 in a matter of weeks!!

Here is another of the many testimonies to...

BRAG ON JESUS

There was a young couple with a large amount of debt who agreed with God's plan to pay off their debt. They had an opportunity for overtime and said **YES** to God's invitation to pay down their debt.

In 4 months, they paid $25,000 of their debt!

You never know how God will work with your YES.

Your YES can move you from financial barrenness and bring you into financing freedom.

BARRENNESS IN OUR BODY

Barrenness is more than the inability to conceive. It can include the lack of the proper anatomy (structure) and physiology (function) in our physical body.

In this story in 2 Kings 4, Elisha encounters a woman who is childless – she is barren. This Shunammite woman and her husband had provided for Elisha every time he came to town. They even built a room for him. Elisha wants to thank her in some way.

> "So, he said, 'What then is to be done for her?' And Gehazi answered, 'Actually, she has no son, and her husband is old.' So he said, 'Call her.' When he had called her, she stood in the doorway. Then he said, 'About this time next year you shall embrace a son.' And she said, 'No, my Lord. Man of God, do not lie to your maidservant!' But the woman conceived, and bore a son when the appointed time had come, of which Elisha had told her." —2 Kings 4:14-17 (NKJV)

There was brokenness and barrenness. This Shunammite woman had settled on never having children. She no longer dreamt of holding a baby in her arms. So, when Elisha spoke of her having a son, it scared her!

Yet one year later this Shunammite woman conceived and gave birth to a son. Not out of her kindness to the prophet —because it is not predicated on her service or devotion to him— but rather on God's responding once again to Elisha's Oneness with the Lord, blessing her with supernatural healing.

LET ME BRAG ON JESUS

I struggled for many years with what was low energy for me and weight gain. The doctors dismissed it as "getting older." Although I played played tennis and ran, I would be exhausted afterwards and still gained weight.

Then one day, I was diagnosed with Hashimoto's disorder and given a very high dose of thyroid medicines. Hashimoto's is an auto-immune disorder that can cause your thyroid not to make enough thyroid hormones and to produce antibodies to attack and kill your thyroid cells.

One day I looked online for a picture of a healthy thyroid, and then I began to visualize mine as healthy, just like the picture.

I knew God was healing me. I searched for my solution in the Word.

My declaration became:

If I declare a thing, it will be established for me. (Paraphrased Job 22:28)

As I think in my heart, therefore I am, with a new thyroid. (Paraphrased Proverbs 23:7)

I continued to declare, "I will prosper and be in good health." (paraphrased 3 John 1:20)

One morning, when I was back in my comfy chair, having my time with the Lord — it happened! The Lord spoke to me, saying, He had healed my thyroid!

I asked Jesus if I could quit taking my meds, and He said, "YES!"

I stopped my meds and returned to the doctor and the tests results confirmed I was healed.

Since then I have been able to lose weight. My energy levels have increased to being able to play tennis in 90-degree heat for three and a half hours.

Praise God! Praise God!

Don't get discouraged over the timing of your breakthrough because God will restore what we've lost. He's also going to use your declarations, your tenacity, your contending, your waiting, your prayers, and your worship to bring everything into alignment for you to receive all the He's going to do for you.

ACTIVATION

What needs redeeming in you to become fruitful?

Do you have something God can multiply to bring you out of the lack?

What needs healing in your body?

You may not have the answers to these questions.

It is an invitation for you to seek the Lord and let Him show you the new way by studying and un-layering the Scriptures God leads you to.

CHAPTER TWO

NEW ANOINTING

Are you ready for a new anointing?

I woke up one Sunday morning and began seeking God for a fresh word. I didn't have a message to preach, so I said, "Lord, I'd like a fresh word for today."

As soon as I asked, He gave me a vision.

I saw a blank canvas.

Then, I saw a "creative swirl" around it. Somehow, I just knew it was a "creative swirl."

I silently asked, "A creative swirl?"

I didn't even know what that was or what that meant, but I knew God wanted to release a "creative anointing."

As I pondered this vision, immediately, the Lord reminded me of the building of the Tabernacle.

I hurried to find the section in Exodus that spoke to this. God began to highlight different sections of His Word. He talked about the expansive way this creative anointing was released in Exodus; and how it is being released as a new move over His people today.

Let's look at what the Lord highlighted starting with Exodus 31:1-5.

"Then the Lord spoke to Moses saying: 'See, I have called by name Bezalel, the son of Uri, the son of Hur, of the tribe of Judah. And I have filled him with the Spirit of God in wisdom, in understanding, in knowledge and in all manner of workmanship, to design artistic works, to work in gold, in silver, in bronze, in cutting jewels for setting, in carving wood and to work in all manner of workmanship.'" (NKJV)

As I read this, I was astounded!

God equipped Bezalel from the inside—Filling him with the Spirit so that he could complete the physical work of building the Tabernacle.

First, God filled Bezalel with His Spirit. The Word says the Spirit searches the deep things of God and reveals them to us. The Spirit living in Bezalel provided close communication with God. Bezalel could now follow the plans to fulfill his purpose because of the new anointing.

Next, God imparted to him what I call the "power package" — Wisdom, Understanding, and Knowledge.

God filled Bezalel with the Holy Spirit to partner with Him. Then, He imparted the "power package," which enabled him to operate in a revelatory level beyond his natural ability. When we receive the "power package," wisdom, understanding, and knowledge, it becomes the spiritual filter in discerning the things of the natural.

Finally, Bezalel was anointed to design and work with various metals, jewels, and woods. He was given skills to create and produce artistic works with an assortment of building materials.

He was not only the architect, but the engineer and builder. God fully equipped him with a new anointing.

Bezalel's new anointing was followed by his new assignment. He was given a 3 step process to complete the work:

1. Hear the instructions

2. Receive what God was giving him

3. Activate it by being obedient to the instructions

Bezalel operated in his anointing to design, create, and build the Tabernacle.

Exodus 35 tells us that in addition to all of that, God added to his assignment, and Bezalel received the ability to teach others.

He directed every engraver, tapestry worker, and all the artisans in their work. In addition, he could teach them what God had anointed him to do. He would pass it on so they could build the Tabernacle.

The Word says in Matthew 10:8, "Freely you have received, freely give."

When we receive from God, we can teach, impart, and pass on to others.

Recently, God has been showing me new anointings. They are out there floating in the air, ready to be pulled down and imparted into people. God has me reach up, grab the anointing, and release it into them.

FYI—anyone can do this—God can open your eyes to see the anointing and to whom it belongs.

He also highlights those who are about to receive a new anointing, as well as people who have received a new anointing, with their assignment sandwiched right into it.

God is highlighting so many new assignments with new anointings outside our realm of understanding and our norm.

He is also giving us the ability to impart, teach, and activate others. Everyone is moving into positions to work for the Kingdom at this designated time.

You may look at something that He's calling you to do and say,

"I don't have any skill for that. I don't have any anointing for this."

Know this, if God is calling you to do it, He's going to equip you to complete the assignment.

Bezalel had God's anointing. He had his assignment. He followed the Lord's leading to design, build, and create the Tabernacle. He used the plans that the Lord gave Moses.

Bezalel heard, received, and activated what God had entrusted him to do.

I feel pushback from some of you, and the pushback is not going to work. I know some of you are shying away from this revelation because you do not believe you are creative. However, let me share a personal story about being creative.

My mom was an artist. She could paint with all different mediums. In addition, she was an amazing seamstress. I remember when she designed and sewed dresses for an entire wedding party—bridesmaids' dresses, and the bride's dress.

I compared my lack of abilities, like painting, designing, and sewing, to my mom's, and as a result I believed I was not creative. But then I learned to receive the truth of who I was, and I began to try different creative outlets.

I share this to encourage you to press through the lies.

This word applies to you. You are creative!

It is your choice if you are going to follow His new way by receiving and activating the anointing of the new move.

What I mean by this, is you can choose to say "yes" to God, even though you don't understand where He is going to take you.

This really boils down to—Do I trust God, especially in the unknown?

Kris Vallotton has taught about prophetic foretelling in the following.

He said that so many times, things are prophesied over us that we don't have the understanding or capacity to do. So, we reject the prophecy because it is too far beyond our current ability.

We walk away from a prophetic foretelling and impartation, saying they missed it this time, there is no way, or I don't have the ability, so it was not a word for me.

One specific example he shared was when he prophesied over someone about being a worship leader and playing an instrument. She replied that she didn't play an instrument and that she was not a worship leader.

Kris replied, "I'm not calling you for who you are now. I'm calling you for the things God has for you to become."

When prophecy is released, either through the Word or through the Prophet, we must hear, receive, and activate the Word.

Keep in mind God calls you to a bigger anointing so you can grow into it.

That Word that is stirring in your Spirit is inviting you to say, "YES."

Lord, give me whatever You have to anoint me, equip me, and finance me for what you want me to accomplish. Show me how, Lord!

ACTIVATION

Ask the Lord, "Is there a word You have spoken to me that I have failed to receive and activate?"

Write down what He is saying.

1. Follow these action steps and get ready to move into the call of God.

2. Repent for not following through

3. Declare: "I receive the assignment You have revealed to me.

4. Take a step of faith to activate what You have declared."

NEW ANOINTING FOR CONSUMING THE WORD

Read the Word.

Consume the Word until it consumes you.

Believe the Word.

Act on the Word.

—Smith Wigglesworth[1]

There are times when we are looking for *something*—direction, anointing, assignment, purpose through everything and everyone.

Then, we have this realization; God is the *something*.

Let's take a look at Ezekiel's anointing from the Lord.

"Like the appearance of a rainbow in a cloud on a rainy day, so was the appearance of the brightness all around it. This was the appearance of the likeness of the glory of the Lord. So, when I saw it, I fell on my face, and I heard a voice of one speaking."—Ezekiel 1:28 (NKJV)

He continues on: "And he said to me, son of man, stand on your feet and I will speak to you. Then the Spirit entered me, and he spoke to me and set me on my feet. And I heard him who spoke to me."—Ezekiel 2:1-2 (NKJV)

As with Bezalel, the Spirit entered Ezekiel, and Ezekiel heard what the Lord was saying to him.

1 (https://www.inspiringquotes.us/author/3141-smith-wigglesworth)

"Moreover, he said to me, 'Son of man, eat what you find; eat this scroll, and go speak to the house of Israel.' So I opened my mouth, and He caused me to eat that scroll.

"And He said to me, 'Son of man, feed your belly, and fill your stomach with this scroll that I give you.' So I ate, and it was in my mouth like honey in sweetness.

"Then he said to me: 'Son of man, go to the house of Israel, and speak with my words to them for you are not sent to a people of unfamiliar speech and of hard language, but to the house of Israel, not too many people of unfamiliar speech and of hard language, whose words you cannot understand. Surely had, I sent you to them, they would have listened to you. But the house of Israel will not listen to you, because they will not listen to Me'." —Ezekiel 3:1-7 (NKJV)

The Lord gives Ezekiel the anointing, assignment, and direction. Ezekiel was given a formidable task; he was to turn the hearts of the house of Israel back to the Lord.

Ezekiel was anointed by the Spirit for his new assignment.

He heard, received, and activated the assignment by consuming the Word.

When I begin to read (consume) the Word, it lights me up inside.

It stirs me into the very presence of God in me.

Consuming the Word takes me to a face-to-face encounter with Him.

It puts His signature inside of me, who He is, what He is saying. And His very breath begins to flow through me.

New anointings are released as you consume the Word.

We live out of the Word of God.

Consuming and living out of the Word changes your very DNA, transforming you into His image. Diffusing it into your cellular memory, which shapes your day to day.

Consuming the Word becomes the very life and breath of these new anointings, new assignments, and new ways God is moving.

With our anointing and new the assignment, we're receiving: not everything will be a hop, skip or jump through the park. We may have to do hard things. But in doing the hard things, God is with us. He has planned for us to break through the hard things.

As we follow Him, we can walk in the fuller measure of the anointing that He's given us.

We understand the new way, and the new anointing, are given for His purpose.

I really want to emphasize this "consuming of the Word."

Jeremiah states,

"Your words were found, and I ate them.
And your Word was to me the joy, and the rejoicing
of my heart;
For I am called by your name,
Oh Lord, God of host." — Jeremiah 15:16 (NKJV)

DECLARATION:

I consume the Word.

The Word overtakes me.

The Word is my very life and breath.

CHAPTER THREE

NEW ASSIGNMENT

Are you ready to be Activated into YOUR NEW ASSIGNMENT?

God is releasing new assignments, and He has one for you!

LET ME BRAG ON JESUS

I want to encourage you with my testimony about being activated for my new assignment.

It was probably 20 years ago, and I was dreaming with God about what I wanted to do in the future. I used to say, "God, whatever You want, that is what I want."

One day He challenged me to begin dreaming about what I wanted.

I began brainstorming with God and keeping a journal of everything that came to mind. One of these was having a TV show. I wanted to be a "Christian Oprah" and reach the masses for Jesus.

I remember when I shared that dream with my mentor He responded, "You are too old for TV. You need to let that go and find something else."

Now remember, that was twenty years ago.

God knew what was in my heart, and He sent me confirmation after confirmation about having a TV show.

About six years ago, I even did a mini YouTube show where I interviewed people, and I loved it!

Fast forward to Fall of 2021, I received the following word:

In Jesus's name, Pastor Cindy, there's a new assignment for you. There's a new assignment for you, but it's not for you alone.

This is what I heard:

There's an apostolic and prophetic remnant that God has called you to that are literally gonna take the airwaves.

I see God opening doors for studio time—Air time— and you're gonna be over all types of media, social media, Christian television —it's going to go out over the airwaves—

It is a strategic assignment for the region and for the nation.

It wasn't long after I received this word that the station director at a Christian TV station invited me to do a weekly TV show.

It was a dream in my heart, and even though my mentor said I was too old twenty years ago, God was saying, "Here, let me fill your heart's desire to make Me known."

And oh, by the way, dreaming with God about what He wanted for my life gave me a beginning for my third book, *God's Dream for Your Life.*

Just as God activated my new assignment, He is readying your new assignment to be activated!

Declare: I am ready for my new assignment to come to life!

Small Assignments

There is a drought in the land of Israel. Elijah leaves the supernatural provision of the Lord where he drank from the brook and ravens supplied him with food, to go to a widow in Zarephath.

There, the Lord had planned for a widow to provide for him.

The Lord tells Elijah,

"Arise, go to Zarephath, which belongs to Sidon,

and dwell there. See, I have commanded a widow there to provide for you." —1 Kings 17:9 (NKJV)

When Elijah arrives, he meets the widow and asks for a drink of water and a bite of bread.

"So she said, 'As the LORD your God lives, I do not have bread, only a handful of flour in a bin, and a little oil in a jar; and see, I am gathering a couple of sticks that I may go in and prepare it for myself and my son, that we may eat it, and die.'" —1 Kings 17:12 (NKJV)

The Lord sent Elijah to a place of provision where there was no provision in the natural.

How can that be possible?

Remember, the Lord had told Elijah that He had commanded the widow to provide for him. Because the widow had nothing to give him, she did not connect Elijah's arrival with the word of the Lord.

Seeing the widow is in a place of desperation and hopelessness, Elijah begins to give her directions.

God sent Elijah to activate the widow's new assignment — providing for him.

Sometimes God gives us an assignment like He did with the widow —one for which we have...

No Vision

No Provision

No Understanding

Only an obedient heart

"And Elijah said to her, 'Do not fear; go and do as you have said, but make me a small cake from it first, and bring it to me; and afterward make some for yourself and your son. For thus says the LORD God of Israel: 'The bin of flour shall not be used up, nor shall the jar of oil run dry, until the day the LORD sends rain on the earth.'

"So she went away and did according to the word of Elijah; and she and he and her household ate for many days. The bin of flour was not used up, nor did the jar of oil run dry, according to the word of the LORD which He spoke by Elijah." —1 Kings 17:13-16 (NKJV)

Notice that the widow had one small assignment, to fix Elijah something to eat. Her assignment seems insignificant and even impossible because she only has a handful of flour in a jar and a little olive oil in a jug.

In the widow's obedience to the assignment, God changed everything!

OBEDIENCE BRINGS BREAKTHROUGH

When we have a breakthrough, we carry an anointing for others to have breakthrough. Our breakthrough becomes an open door for others.

Your **YES** will change your life and the lives of others and build the Kingdom.

Just as a reminder, God didn't give the widow a complete understanding of what or how it would work. But Elijah did tell her what to do step-by-step so she could follow the instructions and complete her assignment.

OUT OF THE WILDERNESS INTO THE NEW ASSIGNMENT

When you think you do not have a future, remember: just like the widow, God has your new assignment.

God will bring you out of the wilderness into your new assignment.

Elijah had gone from the most significant victory to utter despair. He had won an incredible victory over the gods of Baal. Only out of his victory came the news that Jezebel had put a bounty on his head, which sent him into despair.

> "Then Jezebel sent a messenger to Elijah, saying, 'So let the gods do to me, and more if I do not make your life as the life of one of them by tomorrow about this time.'" — 1 Kings 19:2,(NKJV)

Elijah was spiritually, emotionally, and physically exhausted. Terrified, He RAN FOR HIS LIFE.

He had run in fear and then realized he was no better than his fathers and became so greatly discouraged that he prayed to the Lord to take his life.

He believed the lie that there was no hope for him to live.

Elijah heard and believed the assignment of death and destruction that Jezebel had waged against him.

But God wasn't finished with Elijah. God met with Elijah in his despair. He gave him supernatural provision by way of an angel to strengthen him.

Have you been in a season where the weight of discouragement overwhelms you?

I know I have. It usually happens after I experience a powerful move of God. The enemy begins to taunt me with lies of doubt, isolation, and inadequacies. He wants us to run, hide, and not move forward with our calling. We know the enemy wants to kill, steal, and destroy our assignments, lives, and legacy!

But God crashes in to lift us – just as he did with Elijah.

"Then He said, 'Go out, and stand on the mountain before the LORD.' And behold, the LORD passed by, and a great and strong wind tore into the mountains and broke the rocks in pieces before the LORD, but the LORD was not in the wind; and after the wind an earthquake, but the LORD was not in the earthquake; and after the earthquake a fire, but the LORD was not in the fire; and after the fire a still small voice.

"So it was, when Elijah heard it, that he wrapped his face in his mantle and went out and stood in the entrance of the cave. Suddenly a voice came to him, and said, 'What are you doing here, Elijah?' —1 Kings 19:11-13 (NKJV)

This is very interesting!

There are all these manifestations of power, wind, fire, and an earthquake, but God wasn't found in any of those signs.

God was found in the gentle whisper in Elijah's ear asking,

"What are you doing here, Elijah?" —1 Kings 19:13

The Lord's presence moves Elijah from a place of discouragement and despair into a new assignment.

"Then the LORD said to him: 'Go, return on your way to the Wilderness of Damascus; and when you arrive, anoint Hazael as king over Syria. Also you shall anoint Jehu the son of Nimshi as king over Israel. And Elisha the son of Shaphat of Abel Meholah you shall anoint as prophet in your place.' —1 Kings 19:15-16 (NKJV)

Elijah found his next assignment—Elisha—and he threw his mantle over him, indicating a *new assignment* for Elisha.

Elisha followed Elijah.

Still, Elijah did not complete the other two directives the Lord gave him—the anointing of Hazael as King of Syria and the anointing of Jehu as King of Israel.

Both of these new assignments were delayed, leaving Elisha with the task of completing the instructions of the Lord.

Delayed Assignments

We read in 1 Kings 19:16 that Elijah was to anoint Jehu as King of Israel, yet he did not complete his assignment and this caused Jehu's new assignment as King to be delayed for approximately 24 years.

Our new assignments can be delayed at the hands of someone else's disobedience.

Because of Elijah's disobedience, Elisha was the one to complete the word over Jehu so the prophecy of the Lord would be fulfilled. God will accomplish what He wants even if we are disobedient.

> "And when he arrived, there were the captains of the army sitting; and he said, 'I have a message for you, Commander.'

"Jehu said, 'For which one of us?'

"And he said, "For you, Commander."Then he arose and went into the house. And he poured the oil on his head, and said to him, "Thus says the LORD God of Israel: 'I have anointed you king over the people of the LORD, over Israel. You shall strike down the house of Ahab your master, that I may avenge the blood of My servants the prophets, and the blood of all the servants of the LORD, at the hand of Jezebel. For the whole house of Ahab shall perish; and I will cut off from Ahab all the males in Israel, both bond and free." —2 Kings 9:5-8 (NKJV)

Jehu was anointed for his new assignment after 24 years of waiting!

The spiritual impartation was complete. It was up to Jehu to take action now by stepping into his new position as king.

EVERY NEW ASSIGNMENT REQUIRES ACTIVATION

"Then Jehu came out to the servants of his master, and one said to him, 'Is all well? Why did this madman come to you?'

"And he said to them, 'You know the man and his babble.'

"And they said, 'A lie! Tell us now.'

"So he said, 'Thus and thus he spoke to me, saying, 'Thus says the LORD: "I have anointed you king over Israel."'"

"Then each man hastened to take his garment and put it under him on the top of the steps; and they blew trumpets, saying, 'Jehu is king!' —2 Kings 9:11-13 (NKJV)

Jehu hesitated to share he was anointed king because it was an act of treason and he knew he could be killed.

Joram, the son of Ahab, was the King of Israel when Jehu was anointed as the King of Israel.

Except God had a plan to rid Israel of the evil reign of the house of Ahab—and Jehu was it!

Jehu had peers surrounding him who recognized the anointing of God. They celebrated the promotion and stood with Jehu to give him the boldness, courage, and encouragement to step into his new assignment.

"Now when Jehu had come to Jezreel, Jezebel heard of it; and she put paint on her eyes and adorned her head, and looked through a window. Then, as Jehu entered at the gate, she said, 'Is it peace, Zimri, murderer of your master?'

"And he looked up at the window, and said, 'Who is on my side? Who?' So two or three eunuchs looked out at him. Then he said, 'Throw her down.' So they threw her down, and some of her blood spattered on the wall and on the horses; and he trampled her underfoot." —2 Kings 9:30-33 (NKJV)

Jehu used his authority, and at his word Jezebel was taken out.

There are two points I want to make here.

1. God anoints you with authority for your new assignment.

2. God will raise people to stand with you and support you in your new assignment.

LET ME BRAG ON JESUS

Let me share a short testimony about a new assignment God gave me, along with my husband and a friend, to plant a church.

Many years ago, I heard the Lord tell me to get ordained. I had worked in the business world all my life, and I couldn't figure this out. In my obedience I was ordained in 2009.

Once I was ordained, I kept getting words about starting a church, in spite of my lack of interest.

It was like flipping on a switch in a dark room. One day we could not see or comprehend what we were hearing, then suddenly, it all became clear, and we stepped into our new assignment.

We knew for certain when the Word of the Lord came to us all.

We knew the timing for the prophecies was now. We could agree, receive, and step into our new assignment.

One day, you are a widow preparing for your family to die — in a flash, your new assignment is to be the provider for the man of God as he prepares for his next assignment.

One day, you are a commander in the army, the next day, you are the King of Israel in your new assignment ridding Israel of the evil reign.

I believe you have had confirming prophetic words spoken over you for a new assignment.

God wants to release supernatural provision, end delay, and anoint you for your new assignment.

As you read this, God is stirring the new assignment in you.

DECLARATIONS

I declare my lack will turn into supernatural provision for my new assignment.

I declare that I will be obedient to the Word of God.

I declare there will be no more delay in my new assignment.

I declare that others will surround me to support my new assignment.

CHAPTER FOUR

PIONEERING SPIRIT

Are you ready to be a Pioneer?

God has been talking to me about a pioneering spirit that He's releasing. A pioneer opens up a new line of thought or method; they develop something new and prepare the way for others to follow.

God has released a pioneering spirit over His people. He calls us to break new territory, dig up new ground, and create new paths. Preparing the way for others to follow. I believe releasing anointed pioneers is part of God's new move.

It is a new move for all who are willing to receive.

God has designed His family not to merely survive, but to thrive. He is anointing us to not only be the solution makers, but also pioneers. Subsequently, when things get tough, we can pioneer new ways rather than retreat.

God wants us to get out of our familiar pathways and engage in His new way of doing things. He desires us to live Spirit-to-spirit, bringing down heavenly solutions.

When we look at the history of what God has prophetically spoken, it helps us to understand the activation of the seasons.

This deposit of the pioneer spirit we are now working in became available almost 50 years ago. Sometimes, we fail to recognize what is happening, and then there is a "suddenly," and all the pieces come together.

What is available to us now is a fulfillment of the prophetic word and prayer others have labored over making it available for us to reap what others have sown.

> "One sows and another reaps. I sent you to reap that for which you have not labored; others have labored, and you have entered into their labors."
> —John 4:37-38 (NKJV)

LET ME BRAG ON JESUS

When we planted our church, The Gathering with Jesus, the Lord told us what city and showed us where we were to plant. He gave us a specific area.

We did not live in Tarpon Springs. It was not in our sphere of influence or our usual travel route. Nevertheless, God sent us there and told us we would "reap where you did not sow."

As we looked for a building, if we went too far in any direction, the Lord would redirect us. He would not let us move from the triangular area He had assigned us.

Amazingly, another church in the designated area offered to share their building with us. However, within four months, we found our own building, refurbished the entire interior, and moved. All without any debt! We were overwhelmed by God and how clearly, He directed and provided for us.

We were pioneers in a new territory. Since our launch, we have added Prophetic Night (everyone who comes gets a prophetic word), The Outpouring (where we wait on the Holy Spirit), a children's program, an accredited Bible College, and the Supernatural School of Activation to equip pioneers for their sphere of influence. At the time of writing this book, we are preparing to open an elementary school to prepare the upcoming generations to be Kingdom Builders.

Chris Reed, the lead pastor of MorningStar Ministries, said, and I paraphrase, "If you send your children to be taught by Caesar eight hours a day, you can't expect them not to turn out like Romans."

We are building a place where children can mature, knowing their God without restrictions and having a biblical worldview. They will grow in their identity and purpose and become world-changers for the generations to come.

A BIRTHING OF THE PIONEERING SPIRIT

In 1975, Dr. Bill Bright, the founder of Campus Crusade for Christ, and Loren Cunningham, who founded YWAM, met in Colorado. Here is an excerpt from their meeting, taken from Loren Cunningham's book, *Making Jesus Lord*.

> "Sometimes God does something dramatic to get our attention. That's what happened to me in 1975. My family and I were enjoying the peace and quiet of a borrowed cabin in the Colorado Rockies. I was stretched out on a lounge chair in the midday warmth, praying and thinking. I was considering how we Christians—not just the mission I was part of, but all of us—could turn the world around for Jesus."
>
> "A list came to my mind: categories of society which I believed we should focus on in order to turn nations around to God. I wrote them down and stuck the paper in my pocket.
>
> "The next day, I met with a dear brother, the leader of Campus Crusade for Christ, Dr. Bill Bright. He

shared with me something God had given him—
several areas to concentrate on to turn the nations
back to God! They were the same areas, with
different wording here and there, that were written
on the page in my pocket. I took it out and showed
Bill, and we shook our heads in amazement."

"Here's a list (refined and clarified a bit over
the years) that God gave me that sunny day in
Colorado:

1. The home

2. The church

3. Schools

4. Government and politics

5. The media

6. Arts, entertainment, and sports

7. Commerce, science, and technology

"These seven spheres of influence will help us
shape societies for Christ."[2]

The mandate is to bring godly change to nations by
reaching the seven spheres of influence, also known as the
Seven Mountains of influence. But the whole vision is to
transform a nation by becoming an influencer in the sphere
of influence. God puts us in a sphere to influence, some-

2 Making Jesus Lord by Loren Cunningham (YWAM, 1988, p. 134)

times even multiple spheres to influence, and bring His Kingdom into those areas.

My spheres of influence are my Home, Church, Business, and Media.

Where are your spheres of influence God has positioned you?

In the mid 90's, the church I was attending had someone come from YWAM and teach this very thing, the 7 Mountains of Influence. She took us through the Scriptures that supported the prophetic vision God had given Cunningham and Bright. She sowed a seed for the future activation of this prophetic word. Timing of the activation can depend on the soil condition of where the seed is planted. While the seed didn't grow until I left that church, it has flourished since we planted our church in 2012.

As we walk in the vision, God has transitioned us into a position of influence in these areas. And we have watched as God prepares others for a fuller understanding of becoming influencers.

God has set us up to overcome the darkness in these strategic areas and regain power and influence for the Kingdom. We have been sent to influence the decisions made at the top. This doesn't always require that we have to be at the top of the mountain, only influence their decisions.

LET ME BRAG ON JESUS

I was on the Board of an organization that focused on mentoring school students. They began working with a Middle School that had multiple issues.

The Sheriff said, "It was kind of a shock to the senses. I came in thinking, 'How bad can this be? I was in the Middle School once.' I wasn't here on campus but 30 minutes and there was already a huge fight breaking out in the main office."

They invited us to have a weekly prayer time at the school. The team would arrive before anyone else and seek God for a solution and breakthrough for this school.

These are the statistics before we began praying:

850 Students on the Rolls

698 Reported incidents last year

53 incidents reported to the police

Survey revealed only 25% feel safe

After only 5 months of Prayer:

Only 2 incidents reported to the police
(there would have been 26 by this time)

Attendance rate went up to 93%

Two of the most difficult students had turned around and were now helping others.

Teachers and staff were now able to focus more on education rather than settling disputes.[3]

The principal related in a letter that for the first time in many years, she could wear a dress to school because she didn't have to break up fights anymore.

A time of prayer and petition by two to three people each week completely transformed the atmosphere.

That is the power of our God! He opened the door to influence and changed the education mountain, which in turn influenced the family mountain.

Because of the success and victory at this school, the organization was invited into a joint partnership with the County to bring transformation to the largest low-income housing development in the area. The goal was to teach life and parenting skills, finances, and job placement to the providers who worked with these families.

We moved from being bystanders to becoming pioneers with radical influence in the school, family, and government mountains, culminating with the Kingdom of God taking back dominion in those areas.

This Pioneer anointing is available for you right now, and God is ready to activate you. God wants to use you to transform darkness into light and give people a hope and a future. Whether you work in a hospital, an office building, or from your home, it doesn't make any difference.

---

3 City Plan School Project, CityPlan.TV

I know there is such a power wave for this anointing that is happening right now. God is moving. The demonic forces are trembling because they are terrified of the power of God released through His people.

CARRYING THE PIONEERING SPIRIT

Daniel carried the pioneering spirit. He was in a difficult position. He, along with his friends, had been taken from their land and held captive by the King of Babylon. They were young, good-looking, gifted, and quick learners.

Daniel had committed his ways to the Lord in the early days of his captivity.

> "But Daniel purposed in his heart that he would not defile himself with the portion of the King's delicacies, nor with the wine which he drank; therefore he requested of the chief of the eunuchs that he might not defile himself. Now God had brought Daniel into the favor and goodwill of the chief of the eunuchs." —Daniel 1:8-9 (NKJV)

How are you responding to your difficult circumstances?

Daniel set his heart toward what would please God. If he moaned and complained, those attitudes are not reflected in the Word. Daniel set himself up to trust God with the challenges he faced.

Daniel's heart response invited God to shower him with favor and goodwill. Those two words translate very differently in Hebrew than you would think.

Favor is mercy, kindness, goodness, and lovingkindness.

Goodwill is tender love and compassion.

God stirred the chief eunuch to have eyes of loving kindness and tender love for Daniel. His generosity toward Daniel gives him more influence on others and, subsequently, the King.

> "And the chief of the eunuchs said to Daniel, 'I fear my lord the king, who has appointed your food and drink. For why should he see your faces looking worse than the young men who are your age? Then you would endanger my head before the king.'" —Daniel 1:10 (NKJV)

The chief eunuch agreed to allow them to try the food restrictions for 10 days. At the end of the trial period, they looked healthier than all the other young men!

Then God equipped the four men to influence the different kings they would serve.

> "As for these four young men, God gave them knowledge and skill in all literature and wisdom; and Daniel had understanding in all visions and dreams." —Daniel 1:17 (NKJV)

King Nebuchadnezzar found them to be 10 times better than all the rest! Get this—10 Times BETTER!

Are you 10 TIMES better than the non-believers around you?

If not, commit your current assignment to God. Then, ask God for an increased anointing—10 TIMES better than all the rest!

Remember, God anointed you to excel in the realm of influence He has put you in!

DEATH OR PROMOTION

King Nebuchadnezzar had a dream that troubled him. He called his spiritual guides together, which included Daniel, and told them he needed an understanding.

> "The king answered and said to the Chaldeans, 'My decision is firm: if you do not make known the dream to me, and its interpretation, you shall be cut in pieces, and your houses shall be made an ash heap. However, if you tell the dream and its interpretation, you shall receive from me gifts, rewards, and great honor. Therefore tell me the dream and its interpretation.'" —Daniel 2:5-6 (NKJV)

Not only did the King order them to interpret the dream and interpret the content, He ordered them to be put to death if they didn't. The response of the of magicians and astrologers was—THIS IS IMPOSSIBLE!

Daniel's next step is so crucial for us to learn.

He gathers the others, Hananiah, Mishael, and Azariah, to seek God with him for the interpretation of the dream. Like Daniel, when faced with insurmountable circumstances, we must gather our trusted team and pray.

By doing this, many things are accomplished.

A hedge of protection is created, clarity comes, and we are drawn into unity with others in the spiritual realm.

> "Then the secret was revealed to Daniel in a night vision. So Daniel blessed the God of heaven."
> —Daniel 2:19 (NKJV)

Then, Daniel introduces King Nebuchadnezzar to the ...

> "God in heaven who reveals secrets." — Daniel 2:28 (NKJV)

Remember, God's Word says that the Holy Spirit searches the deep things of God and reveals them to us. (1 Corinthians 2) You have access to the deep, secret things of God.

ACCESS AND OWNERSHIP

Recently, I had a vision that I want to share with you. The vision helped me to understand access and ownership. I hope it will help you, too.

Jesus takes me by the hand in the vision, and we enter the heavenly realm.

He tells me, "This is where you reside. Your natural body is on earth, but your spirit dwells with us. This is your home. You have full access."

He shows me different rooms. One specifically was a "Whirlwind" room. There were dark blue swirls around the room, with golden, yellow hues within the swirls. The room reminded me of Van Gogh's *Starry Night* painting.

The room contained the movement of Heaven on the earth. The swirls were lights illuminating the darkness. In this place, promises are released, and angels are dispatched. It was a staging place for the next cycle of time.

Jesus says, "You have ownership of all that is mine."

I told the Lord, "There is a big difference between access and ownership."

He reminded me that everything He has belongs to us, the family of God.

I thought about Ephesians 1:3, "Blessed be the God and Father of our Lord Jesus Christ, who has blessed us with every spiritual blessing in the heavenly places in Christ."

As with Daniel, we have that same ability to *access* the fullness of God's answers to everything we need. We have *ownership* of heaven's secrets, and God wants to give us the keys to unlock the solutions for our sphere of influence.

After Daniel shared the revelation with King Nebuchadnezzar, he received the highest promotion as Ruler over the Province of Babylon. And he became the Chief over all the wise men.

When you are the only one with the answer to a question that no one else can answer, you will be promoted—as the one above all others.

God will give you access to the answers to your problems you encounter.

His Word says,

"These kingdom revelations will break open your understanding to unveil the deeper meaning of parables, poetic riddles, and epigrams, and to unravel the words and enigmas of the wise." —Proverbs 1:6 (TPT)

LET ME BRAG ON JESUS

I was ministering at a prophetic conference. I had a word for a gentleman. After he received the word, he shared what the Lord was doing, which confirmed what I had prophesied over him.

Here's his testimony:

He lives and owns a business in New Jersey. And he said

in the last two and a half years, during COVID, God has multiplied my business even though New Jersey had one of the tightest restricted states. During the lockdown, he had prospered. He said that his business had grown so much that it enabled him to buy additional work trucks for cash and a house.

What happened in his business goes against logic. During the lockdown, when many were financially strapped, he prospered. While many businesses failed, he grew his business, and while many lost their homes he was able to buy a house.

Agree with God that this testimony will become yours.

And you will prosper and grow where God has placed you!

Oppression brings out the Fierceness in Pioneers

All of Babylon was commanded to bow down and worship the gold image the King had made. If anyone did not, they would be thrown into a fiery furnace and burned alive.

Shadrach, Meshach, and Abed-Nego, the men of God, would not bend their knees to a pagan idol. This enraged King Nebuchadnezzar.

"But if you do not worship, you shall be cast immediately into the midst of a burning fiery furnace. And who is the god who will deliver you from my hands?" —Daniel 3:15 (NKJV)

The fierceness of Shadrach, Meshach, and Abed-Nego arose as they responded to the King.

"O Nebuchadnezzar, we have no need to answer you in this matter. If that is the case, our God whom we serve is able to deliver us from the burning fiery furnace, and He will deliver us from your hand, O king. But if not, let it be known to you, O king, that we do not serve your gods, nor will we worship the gold image which you have set up." —Daniel 3:16-18 (NKJV)

They were not impressed by the King's threats. Whether God rescued them or not, they would not be oppressed and forced to worship idols. They would only bow down and worship God, regardless of what it cost them—even their life!

Like others before him, Daniel and his friends were pioneering new roads to make way for others in the generations. They demonstrated boldness, fierceness, and commitment to God and only God.

King Nebuchadnezzar sent the three men to the fiery furnace. The furnace was so hot that the flames overtook the guards, killing them.

This is the remarkable, awesome, amazing part.

"Then King Nebuchadnezzar was astonished; and he rose in haste and spoke, saying to his counselors,

'Did we not cast three men bound into the midst of the fire?'

"They answered and said to the king, 'True, O king. Look' he answered, 'I see four men loose, walking in the midst of the fire; and they are not hurt, and the form of the fourth is like the Son of God.'
— Daniel 3:24-25 (NKJV)

Not only were there four men instead of three, but the Son of God formed a supernatural flame-retardant shield around them, and they were no longer bound, but they were freely walking around the flames!

When the King's men came and...

"they saw these men on whose bodies the fire had no power; the hair of their head was not singed nor were their garments affected, and the smell of fire was not on them."—Daniel 3:27 (NKJV)

King Nebuchadnezzar caused Shadrach, Meshach, and Abed-Nego to prosper and promoted them in their sphere of influence.

When God gives you victory in the face of the enemy — expect to prosper with a promotion!

God wants to Build Your Reputation as a Pioneer

God is calling pioneers to break through territory that has not been forged before. In doing so, He is building

67

the reputation of this new breed of pioneers. He is partnering with them in new ideas, solutions, inventions, and strategies that will release the Kingdom into their areas of influence.

These pioneers are becoming a sought-after commodity.

Others need what they carry in the spirit, in the natural.

We have touched on Daniel's influence on the governmental mountain. God had built Daniel's reputation as the only one with the answers to the problems.

In another account, King Belshazzar was having a party for one thousand of his closest friends!

They had raided the House of God and taken the gold vessels from the temple. They drank from them and were praising idols.

Suddenly, a man's hand appeared and the fingers began to write the wall. Terror gripped the King, so much "that the joints of his hips were loosened and his knees knocked against each other." —Daniel 5:6 (NKJV)

The King called all of his wise men to interpret the writing. But none could! God had built Daniel's reputation as the only one with the answers to the problems.

Daniel's track record for unraveling mysteries was unparalleled. No one in the King's court had the wisdom and understanding like Daniel.

The queen remembers this and tells the King:

"There is a man in your Kingdom in whom is the Spirit of the Holy God. And in the days of your father, light and understanding and wisdom, like the wisdom of the gods, were found in him; and King Nebuchadnezzar your father—your father the king—made him chief of the magicians, astrologers, Chaldeans, and soothsayers. Inasmuch as an excellent spirit, knowledge, understanding, interpreting dreams, solving riddles, and explaining enigmas were found in this Daniel, whom the king named Belteshazzar, now let Daniel be called, and he will give the interpretation." — Daniel 5:11-12 (NKJV)

Daniel interpreted the writings on the wall. It was not a good word!

God had judged the King's reign. The King was found to be lacking in his rulership and dies.

Darius takes Belshazzar's place, and Daniel gets another promotion. He was promoted above all others because of the reputation he had built for himself.

"It pleased Darius to set over the kingdom one hundred and twenty satraps, to be over the whole kingdom; Then this Daniel distinguished himself above the governors and satraps, because an excellent spirit was in him; and the king gave thought to setting him over the whole realm."

—Daniel 6:1, 3 (NKJV)

LET ME BRAG ON JESUS

We heard a testimony from a husband and wife who had spent 15 years in a foreign country. They had such an impact they were declared enemies of the state and forced to leave.

They have commissioned and sent 300 missionaries that are passionate about finishing the work they had started. They said their new assignment was to send 'flaming arrows' back into that nation. By doing this, the husband declared their work could not be stopped, and what they sowed would not go to waste.

They are shooting 300 flaming arrows into their sphere of influence, even though they are not physically there. The in-roads of the Kingdom will continue.

Lord, make us flaming arrows for You! Send us as pioneers to transform our spheres of influence.

RELEASING THE PIONEERING SPIRIT

Everyone has one or more spheres of influence, be it your home, church, school, government, media, arts, or business. I encourage you to go out and activate what you have received.

Are you ready to be a **Pioneer?**

Lord,

Impart Your Pioneer Spirit to those seeking. Position and empower them in areas of influence. Enhance their abilities and build their reputations so that they will be sought after. Enable each one to bring solutions no one else can provide. Let them become the brokers of the mysteries, like Daniel, that usher in the Kingdom of God. In Jesus's Name.

CHAPTER FIVE

SEED AND FULFILLMENT

Are you the Prophetic Seed for the Future or Fulfillment of the Past?

Before we get to the essence of this subject, I want to share something I have learned that will enhance your ability to hear and discern what the Lord is doing through you.

I have developed a different way of engaging with the Lord in my quiet time as I read the Word. Since I have learned to read the Word this way, my level of revelation, visions, and encounters with God have increased exponentially.

The Lord has taught me to read until I sense His presence by Him highlighting a particular area. It can be a single word, a phrase within a verse, or several verses. Currently, I am reading Proverbs.

First, I write down what He highlighted. I usually read aloud what I have written down.

Then, I will ask the Lord something like, "What do You have for me today or What do You want to show me?" Then I settle in and wait for His prompting.

The Lord gave me a vision after reading Proverbs 3:16-20 (TPT).

> "Wisdom extends to you long life in one hand and wealth and promotion in the other.
>
> "Out of her mouth flows righteousness, and her words release both law and mercy.
>
> "The ways of wisdom are sweet, always drawing you into the place of wholeness.
>
> "Seeking for her brings the discovery of untold blessings, for she is the healing tree of life to those who taste her fruits. The Lord laid the earth's foundations with wisdom's blueprints. By his living-understanding all the universe came into being.
>
> "By his divine revelation he broke open the hidden fountains of the deep, bringing secret springs to the surface as the mist of the night dripped down from heaven."

I saw the Lord standing in a room, and He extended His hand, inviting me to join Him. The room was a plain beige color. There was no furniture, nothing on the walls —it was completely empty.

(God often shows me things in a way I can understand.)

From here, He took me far above the earth. The sky was deep blue, and the stars brilliantly lit the dark sky. The moon was a small crescent sliver. We went over and sat on the curve of the moon.

I could not take my eyes off the brilliance of the sky. The stars radiated with multi-faceted glimmers of light.

Jesus began to speak.

As He extended His arm, He told me that as far as the sky extends, so is our limitless capacity. He explained how we are invited into an unlimited capacity because we are in Him. Though we seem limited by the natural constraints of the world, our position in the heavenly realm supersedes the restraints.

Immediately, I thought of words the Lord spoke to Abraham in Genesis 15:5.

"Then He brought him outside and said, 'Look now toward heaven, and count the stars if you are able to number them.' And He said to him, 'So shall your descendants be.' And he believed in the LORD, and He accounted it to him for righteousness." (NKJV)

I began to receive words from Jesus. In my mind, I could hear Jesus's thoughts. We were exchanging thoughts mind to mind. So amazing to hear someone think.

What you do in your life affects eternity and the generations to come. Some of what you do will become seed for the next generation, while others will be a fulfillment from the seeds of previous generations.

There are things you do that will be the seed for the next generation.

There are things you do that are the fulfillment of the generation seeds before you.

I was awestruck; His words were so profound.

I asked myself, what am I sowing for future generations, and what am I fulfilling from the past generations?

What are you sowing and fulfilling?

Having looked at Genesis 15:5, let's dig deeper.

Abraham and Sarah are childless. Abram begins to explain to God the problem with his servant being his heir, all because God hadn't given them a son.

It is funny how we explain to God what He needs to do to fix our problem —even though He has written our story. God knows everything, but sometimes we must pour out our hearts, frustrations, and fears to Him. When we do, it clears the clutter from our minds and allows God to speak into the matter.

Here is God's response the Abraham.

"Then He brought him outside and said, "Look now toward heaven, and count the stars if you are able to number them." And He said to him, "So shall your descendants be." — Genesis 15:5 (NKJV)

This word from the Lord took Abraham to a more significant measure of faith. He believed God.

Abraham's word was that his son would be the promised seed for future generations. Abraham didn't understand how his descendants would fill the earth like the stars filled the sky. But he knew God, and when God spoke — he believed!

Abraham and Sarah had one child, Isaac. From their one child came the birthing of a nation. Isaac was their seed for the generations to come.

Think about this:

God's Word was that Abraham and Sarah's descendants would be a many as the stars; their only child would be the seed for fulfilling the generations to come.

Abraham's faith in God and His promise became the open door for us to be the fulfillment from Abraham's one seed, Isaac. From the fulfillment of God's promise, as believers, we can share in Abraham's blessings as our blessing, too!

That's what the Scripture means when it says:

"I have made you the father of many nations."

He is our example and father, for in God's presence he believed that God can raise the dead and call into being things that don't even exist yet. Against all odds, when it looked hopeless, Abraham believed the promise and expected God to fulfill it.

And so the blessing of Abraham's faith is now our blessing too! Romans 4:17-18, Galatians 3:9, (TPT)

FULFILLING AND SEEDING

Again, some of what you do is fulfilling the promises that God gave past generations. Imagine that truth over your life. There have been words spoken and Scripture declared over you that are fulfilling the promises of God. Most of the time, we aren't even aware of what is happening.

The Lord spoke to my mother in much the same way as He did with Abraham. He said, "not one of your children will be lost." We call it the "promise."

I am the fulfillment of that seed spoken to my mom. That word has become the seed for my children and the descendants to come. I pray Isaiah 59:21 over them all the time.

"As for Me," says the LORD, "this is My covenant with them: My Spirit who is upon you, and My words which I have put in your mouth, shall not depart from your mouth, nor from the mouth of your descendants, nor from the mouth of your descendants' descendants," says the LORD, "from this time and forevermore." (NKJV)

Like Abraham, I will not see the fulfillment of all I am seeding while I am on earth. I won't live long enough; one-hundred twenty years will not capture it all. However, I know the promise of God, and it will happen.

There are things that God has promised us that we may not see fulfillment in our lifetime. But, we are planting for generations to come. They will be the fulfillment of our faithfulness to the seed that God has given us.

We think about our day-to-day and all the things that we do. We don't realize the significance or the impact we are making. Every prayer we pray, every stand we take for the Kingdom of God, and, most importantly, walking in our identity and purpose, plants seeds of the promise and fulfills seeds of the promise from others.

There is a Cloud of Witnesses surrounding us, cheering us on because they see the fulfillment of their seeds. One day, we will be part of that great cloud, cheering on the generations that follow.

MOSES FULFILLED THE PROMISE

In Exodus 2, Moses was born at a time when Pharaoh was killing all Hebrew males being born. His mother hid him for three months until she could hide him no longer. She made a basket for him, wrapped him up, and left him at the river bank. Pharaoh's daughter found him and took him in as her own.

Moses was born to be a deliverer of the oppressor of Israel. Israel was oppressed by the very Ruler who raised Moses. Moses would later deliver Israel from their oppressors.

Moses was the fulfillment of the seed, the word, that was planted 400 years prior. God had told Abraham what was going to occur.

"Then He said to Abram: "Know certainly that your descendants will be strangers in a land that is not theirs, and will serve them, and they will afflict them four hundred years. And also the nation whom they serve I will judge; afterward they shall come out with great possessions." —Genesis 15:13-14 (NKJV)

God used Moses to fulfill the promise of deliverance to the house of Israel and to give them the provision of freedom.

We are all created to be deliverers for God and plunderers of what the enemy has taken. Our ability goes back to our committed hearts to God and His plan for us.

LET ME BRAG ON JESUS

I am learning how to have a surrendered heart. My surrender has shifted from "a labor to surrender" to a "love of surrender."

As I moved in this, I didn't know what needed to happen, but I knew God did. I trusted Him to work things out and let me know what I needed to do.

There has been such freedom in surrendering my heart out of love and trust in God completely. I have also found that it frees the Lord to move on my behalf. By my leaning into His best, the outcomes have been mind-blowing.

Here is an example of my surrender and trust.

I scheduled a flight at 6:00 a.m. on a Friday so that I could speak at the conference that night. I arrived at the airport, and my flight was canceled.

I was rebooked for the 6:00 a.m. flight on Saturday morning. Of course, that would not work.

I had a fleeting thought to just call my husband and go home.

Then I thought, *God, I am sure You have this worked out.*

I opened up all the airline apps and began looking at flights. I found one that departed at 7:30 a.m., and I booked it. The cost was almost double!

Then, God stepped in: First, the airlines that bumped me gave me a refund for the non-refundable airfare. At the conference, someone wrote me a sweet card and gave me an envelope full of cash, so my extra cost was covered!

There is an ease of moving with Him when there is a

total surrender to God. It feels like my will has melted down into a loving Oneness with Him.

YOU ARE THE SEED AND THE FULFILLMENT

Moses was the fulfillment of the deliverer of the Israelites from 400 years of captivity. Moses also became the seed for the Promised Land, where Joshua would become the fulfillment.

In Deuteronomy 31, Moses tells the people that he cannot cross the Jordan into the Promise Land. Moses had delivered them from oppression, built the Tabernacle, and was their leader, but he was to become the seed of promise for Joshua to fulfill.

> "Then Moses called Joshua and said to him in the sight of all Israel, 'Be strong and of good courage, for you must go with this people to the land which the LORD has sworn to their fathers to give them, and you shall cause them to inherit it. And the LORD, He is the One who goes before you. He will be with you, He will not leave you nor forsake you; do not fear nor be dismayed.'"
> —Deuteronomy 31:7-8 (NKJV)

Joshua was the leader that would take Israel into the Promised Land.

The word given to Abraham 400 years ago was now fulfilled hundreds of years later by Joshua and the younger generation.

In looking at the lives of Abraham, Isaac, Moses, and Joshua, we see that they were both the seed for future generations and the fulfillment of past promises.

Like those who have gone before us, you are a seed and a fulfillment for the Lord.

The Lord will have you seed the ground, and in a hundred years from now, a generation will harvest what you have planted. And there are things that you are harvesting right now that a generation 50, 100, 200 years ago planted.

PRAYER

Lord, we thank You that we are not only the seed for the future generation, but we are the fulfillment of the generation past. Thank You, Lord, for the great Cloud of Witnesses cheering for us. We thank You, Lord, for the limitless possibilities open to us. We are in awe of Your wonder and Your promise to do immeasurably more than we can ever imagine or dream. You love us with an everlasting love, so we surrender from a heart of love for You. We bless You and honor You, In Jesus's Name, Amen.

CHAPTER SIX

NOT THE WHERE BUT THE WHO

Paul had an assignment to go to Rome and share Jesus Christ with Caesar. (Acts 27, 28) As a prisoner, he was transported by a ship traveling through the treacherous waters of the Mediterranean.

In a fierce storm, the ship began to break apart, and they found themselves swimming for their lives to reach the Isle of Malta. Their stop in Malta was unplanned.

God used the unplanned stop to change the lives of EVERYONE on the island! For a moment, the destination of Rome (THE WHERE) was put on hold so that the people (THE WHO) could encounter God.

Here's a little more of the story.

While warming himself by the fire, a poisonous snake latched on to Paul. He should have dropped dead! But God displayed His supernatural protection over Paul for the islanders to witness. Because of this, Paul received an invitation to visit the leader of Malta. While he was there, he learned the father was sick with dysentery.

> "Paul went in to him and prayed, and he laid his hands on him and healed him." —Acts 28:8 (NKJV)

From that display of God's miracle working power, all who were sick were brought to Paul. They were all healed!

Just like Paul, our destination, the WHERE, can make unexpected stops. When that happens, we need to look for "the WHO."

Two Personal Examples

During my annual review in my early days of corporate management, my boss told me I was great at accomplishing the company's goals. However, in achieving the goals, I left a wake of bodies in the process. I was shocked!

He mentored me through this challenge. It changed my perspective, and I realized that my staff's input was pivotal to achieving the goal.

I learned it wasn't the WHERE, the goal, but the WHO God had put on my team.

Our collaboration enabled us to work more effectively while creating a greater unity with much less drama. I learned that achieving the goal was much smoother when everyone found their role within the goal.

The other example was when I rented a cabin for my sabbatical in the North Georgia mountains. (The WHERE) I had stocked with all the supplies needed so I didn't have to leave, and I could spend time with the Lord.

One morning, the Lord told me to go to Starbucks and meet someone. It was about 20 minutes away. I had no idea who I was meeting. I just knew I had to go.

Arriving at Starbucks, I ordered a coffee and sat down. I looked carefully at everyone who came in, asking the Lord, "Is this the one?" (The WHO)

I met a builder who told me all about the new plans he had developed. But he wasn't the one.

Finally, after a few hours, I decided to leave. As I walked out the door, a couple was coming in. I walked past them. The Lord said, "They're the ones."

I turned around, followed them in, and introduced myself. They were believers and leaders in ministry. God gave me encouragement for them. I prayed for their physical healing and prophesied into their future.

What an amazing time! God interrupted my plans of WHERE to find the WHO.

Distinguishing Who God has Sent

Look around you and note *who* is in your circle of influence. They can be familiar people in your workplace, neighborhood, children's school, or family.

The Who can also be strangers that are set on your path.

Let's start in 2 Kings 6. Elisha and his servant realize the enemy has them surrounded.

> "So when the Syrians came down to him, Elisha prayed to the LORD, and said, 'Strike this people, I pray, with blindness.' And He struck them with blindness according to the word of Elisha."
> —2 Kings 6:18 (NKJV)

Elisha marched the blinded enemy troops inside the gates of Samaria. Next, he commanded their eyes to be open. God opened their eyes, and they saw they were inside Samaria. The King of Israel asked Elisha if he should have them killed.

Elisha's reply was something utterly different from his previous experiences. This new battle required new ways.

Instead of destroying his enemy, Elisha develops an unspoken peace treaty by displaying the mercy of God to the enemy troops. He feeds them, blesses them, and saves them from impending death, creating an unexpected outcome of safety for Israel from any additional attacks.

When we encounter others, friendly or foe, we need to know from the Lord what His plan is for them. We can learn valuable lessons from Elisha's actions.

In this case, Elisha rendered his enemy powerless. He moved them into a place of containment. Next, he blessed them with a meal made especially for the troops and sent them safely home.

Elisha expanded his sphere of influence by following a new move of God, making allies out of his enemies, which enlarged his tribe.

WHO IS YOUR TRIBE?

The buzz phrase in the last ten years has been "finding your tribe." Being part of a tribe is not a new concept in the Kingdom. Throughout Scripture, we find a calling by God to align with others. i.e., tribe, to accomplish a purpose.

Nehemiah deeply desired to rebuild the destroyed walls of Jerusalem. The King gave him permission and favor with others to fulfill his purpose.

Nehemiah could not do this work alone. He had to find his tribe to assist him. He arrived in Jerusalem, surveyed the wall, and shared a vision for rebuilding.

"Then I said to them, 'You see the distress that we are in, how Jerusalem lies waste, and its gates are burned with fire. Come and let us build the wall of

Jerusalem, that we may no longer be a reproach.'"
—Nehemiah 2:17 (NKJV)

The people who caught the vision and felt the call of God volunteered to help rebuild the wall.

"So they said, 'Let us rise up and build.' Then they set their hands to this good work."
—Nehemiah 2:18 (NKJV)

Nehemiah gathered his tribe, and they were ready to go to work. Just a point worth mentioning, not everyone who heard about the vision joined Nehemiah's tribe. In fact, some were against him.

This helps us to realize that there are people specifically called to our Tribe. Not everyone will get behind you in what God has called you to do.

At our church, the Gathering Apostolic Center, it took several years to clarify our assignment. We realized our purpose was to steward the Presence of God and have an impact for the Kingdom through the people God was sending.

Once we had clarity, we began drawing in the right people to help accomplish God's assignment.

Our assignment is to help others gain influence in their spheres of influence, such as the workplace, family, government, and neighborhoods.

We carry an anointing to recognize the move of God and take action. We have seen lives transformed, leaders raised, received favor, debts canceled, and families restored.

God has begun to draw people from other cities and states to be part of our tribe. We have people who drive an hour or more to come each week. Several people moved from another state to be a part of our church family. One of our members even lives in a different country.

LET ME BRAG ON JESUS

The story I am about to share is only a small part of what God did for one of our covenant families.

Two years ago, Michele heard an interview I did on a podcast. She had been looking for people to connect with who wanted to grow spiritually. Michele also wanted to be stretched and fully live in her purpose. She began to follow the Gathering online, read my books, and took the classes via zoom.

Frequently God would have her make the eight-hour drive into town for service. About a year later, the Lord began to talk to her about moving to Florida. It took about nine months for her to find the right job and move.

Here is just one of the many miracles she experienced.

When she moved to Florida, the housing market was at its peak, and her job was in one of the most expensive areas. People told her she would never find affordable housing there.

BUT GOD—within thirty days, she found the perfect place near her job that fit her budget! Her new job far exceeds her previous one. She has so much favor and influence at work and is making an impact there.

In addition, Michele is completing our ministry school and will be ordained at graduation. She has become a vital part of our assignment. And her experience has led others to move and become part of our family.

How do you find your tribe?

1. Seek the Lord to connect you with the right people
2. Invest time in getting acquainted with those God connections
3. Find out how you can add value to their assignment
4. Your tribe's assignment should open up growth opportunities for you

Angels Can Be Your Who

Let's look back at 2 Kings 6; this time, let's look from a different perspective.

Elisha's servant became terrified when he saw the surrounding army. He asked Elisha what they should do.

"So he answered, 'Do not fear, for those who are with us are more than those who are with them.'

"And Elisha prayed, and said, 'LORD, I pray, open his eyes that he may see.' Then the LORD opened the eyes of the young man, and he saw. And behold, the mountain was full of horses and chariots of fire all around Elisha."—2 Kings 6:16-17 (NKJV)

Notice that the Lord sent an army of angels to help Elisha and his servant. They enabled Elisha so he could continue his assignment. We may not see the angels around us, but God has sent them to us.

"God sends angels with special orders to protect you wherever you go, defending you from all harm."—Psalms 91:11 (TPT)

Elisha assured his servant they had the upper hand because God had sent His army. Surrounded and protected by an invisible force of horses and chariots of fire.

God protects us the same way He did Elijah.

ENCOUNTERING ANGELIC ASSISTANCE

I want to share a recent vision that will open your eyes to the angelic assistance God has for us. As you read it, ask the Lord to open your understanding to partner with angelic assistance.

I was having my morning time with the Lord, reading His Word.

As I meditated on the Word, I saw a glimpse of angelic presence fluttering around. I knew the Lord was getting my attention. I asked the Lord, "What would You like to tell me?"

He said, "I have sent an angelic crowd to surround you for what you are doing. There is so much more I want to impart to you. And I want you to teach your people how to impart to others."

I asked the Lord to tell me more about the angelic crowd.

I saw them bunched up around me. It was very much like being on a busy New York City sidewalk, where everyone was crowded together. The angels were in translucent white garments, and everywhere I moved, they moved. We moved as one.

The Lord said, "I have you surrounded. There is much more for you to do; you need My angelic assistance to accomplish it."

Then I saw the angels running interference, whispering downloads, and doing what was needed to accomplish their assignment.

The angels are sent to help me in completing my new assignment.

I asked the Lord about my future assignment.

He responded, "It's not about Where you go — it's about Who you are sent to. You are called to influence, impart, and persuade. You are building, things will change in a moment, and your circle of influence will expand."

ANGELIC ASSISTANCE

This vision the Lord gave me is to open our spiritual senses to the angelic assistance God dispatches. He is sending angels to accompany us to build and expand our influence.

I saw the angels in the vision operating in three areas.

1. Running interference to keep distractions from taking us off track

2. Keeping the enemy at bay

3. Giving informational downloads, thoughts, ideas, and solutions, to assist us in accomplishing our assignment.

PRAYER

Lord, thank You for angelic assistance. Thank You for the unexpected stops so others can encounter Your Glory. Open my eyes to be keenly aware of those You are highlighting for me. I will be available where You send me and to whoever You put in my path. Thank You, Lord!

Chapter 7

VISION FOR LIFE

Preparing for Long Life

"... yet his days shall be one hundred and twenty years."—Genesis 6:3 (NKJV)

Y ou may not have thought about this before—this is God's Word.

If He says we are to live to one-hundred twenty years old, than that is what we have to plan.

> "When there is no clear prophetic vision, people quickly wander astray.But when you follow the revelation of the word, heaven's bliss fills your soul."—Proverbs 29:18 (TPT)

Do you have a vision for your days to one-hundred twenty?

A vision gives us anticipation for the years to come.

Vision fills us with possibilities.

The Lord has a vision for our one-hundred twenty years.

In Jeremiah 29:11, God tells Jeremiah about the future vision for Israel.

> "For I know the plans I have for you," declares the LORD, "plans to prosper you and not to harm you, plans to give you hope and a future." (NIV)

In my book, *God's Dream for Your Life,* I delve into the possibilities of living one-hundred twenty years. I believe we can create a Perfect Health Zone in partnership with God to live to one-hundred twenty. I call it the Moses Principle.

I go into great detail in my book, but let me give you a brief overview. A foundational Scripture is...

> "The secret things belong to the Lord our God, but the things revealed belong to us and to our sons forever, that we may observe all the words of this law." —Deuteronomy 29:29 (NASB)

When the Lord reveals something to us, it is ours to own and live out. Long life is a revelation that the Lord is highlighting for us to expect and experience.

In Deuteronomy 34, Moses is in his final days of life. He had already anointed Joshua to succeed him and take Israel into the Promise Land.

> "Moses was one hundred and twenty years old

when he died. His eyes were not dim nor his natural vigor diminished." —Deuteronomy 34:7 (NKJV)

120 YEAR OLD — and his body was still strong.

Are you ready to live to 120 years old?

My dear friend has a motto about living to 120 years old. She says, "I am living to 120 years old, and I am not going crawling!"

These are the world's stats, not the possibilities in the Kingdom of God.

In 1900's life expectancy was 46 years for men and 48 for women.

In 2022, the life expectancy is 79 years for men and 81 for women.

Based on these world stats, life expectancy has almost doubled in the last 122 years.

But the Kingdom stats look much different when we factor in God and His promises of long life.

If you are 40, you aren't even at mid-life; you still have 80 years to go.

If you are 60, you are just hitting your stride and have 60 more years to go.

If you are 80, you have a solid 40 years to try something bold and courageous.

Let's do the math.

How many years do you have until you reach 120 years old?

If I lived to be 120 years old, it would be possible for me to see my grandchildren's children.

At the time of writing this book my granddaughters are 1, 2, and 4 years old. They have 119, 118, and 116 years to live until they are 120. How exciting!

Think about this in relation to your age.

How many years does that leave you to impact the Kingdom of God?

It's time for you to discover God's dream for your life.

LET ME BRAG ON JESUS

We have friends who are twins, and they just celebrated their one hundredth birthday. They are full of life and filled with the Holy Spirit's fire. Recently, on their way to the store, one of them insisted on stopping by the fire department. She gathered everyone in the firehouse together and told them about Jesus. Several gave their lives to Jesus that day.

Based on the Moses Principle, they have at least 20 more years to impact the Kingdom.

THE LIE WE BELIEVE

We have been sold a bill of goods all of our lives. We were taught that when we retire we are to play golf, travel, grow a garden, enjoying our golden years in a lounge chair with a remote!

I am not saying there is anything wrong with these things. However, God has more extraordinary things for you to do!

He will give you purpose, passion, and a vision for your future.

Rick Joyner of MorningStar Ministries replaced the word 'retirement' with REFIREMENT!

It's time for us to live with a *refirement* for the future.

How Do You Build a Vision for Your Future?

I want to begin by sharing a vision I received from the Lord.

In the vision, I could see the Lord hovering above me. He invited me to come up with Him. As I stood by His side, I saw a fully lit scene in front of us. It seemed to be a road lined with trees and foliage. Everything was vibrant, illuminated with the Lord's glory.

I asked the Lord, "What is this?"

The Lord responded,

"It is a highway of holiness. This is a highway that, once you start down, you cannot go back. Once you step onto the pavement, it will activate a new journey for you. The old will need to be left behind to make room for the new. Do not try to figure out the old; I will show you."

I looked at the Lord with an expression of question, as if to say, "Can I step on the path?"

The Lord explained that these are steps of surrender.

Each step is a step of surrender and with each step He beckons you to go deeper. He is inviting you to a knowing that is so intimate it creates Oneness.

Our Oneness with Him takes us from glory to glory, transforming us into His image.

The Oneness brings you into a bubble of grace to do what you need to do.

Your mind will be opened to receiving new revelation. You will tap into a greater realm in the Spirit. Your focus will be shifted to the things of God.

The Lord brought clarity as He spoke these words.

"This Highway of Holiness invites you into a closer
   relationship with Us.
You will move as We move, and do as We do."

I felt ready and I stepped onto the highway.

I was quite surprised by the unexpected texture of the highway. It wasn't hard and firm like a normal highway. It was fluid, splashy, and fun, and the substance was thick like paint. It splashed up like a water puddle when I stepped onto the highway.

I began to run up and down the highway. As I looked down, the radiance of the highway was splashing this holiness and glory; brightness all over me.

I realized the highway was splashing holiness on me. I sensed that I was walking in the wonder of holiness in God's very presence.

I had seen lots of colors that were tangible. The yellow-gold was majestic—without explanation.

I felt like a child in an unbelievable adventure with the Lord. There was a wonder of Him—what does this really mean? What will this look like as it unfolds? I was filled with gratitude.

I want to invite you to step into the Highway of Holiness and experience all that God has for you.

"A highway shall be there, and a road, and it shall be called the Highway of Holiness."—Isaiah 35:8 (NKJV)

This highway is full of opportunities and possibilities with the Lord. Many things you encounter will be an unexpected surprise of breakthrough that will become part of your everyday life.

LET ME BRAG ON JESUS

I have experienced unexpected breakthroughs that have become part of my everyday life. God has released an ability to call an end to delays and experience early deliveries. This ability is transferable to you.

The breakthrough came in the Summer of 2021. I had ordered a couch, and they said it would not arrive until 2022. I told the Lord, "That isn't going to work for me. I need it before Thanksgiving." Within weeks, they called and asked if they could deliver the couch —5 months early!

I shared this testimony at another church; someone had been waiting for their couch for seven months. They declared the end to the delay, and the couch came within that same month.

I had ordered a shirt for my son for Christmas, and the delivery was scheduled December 24. I received a notice that it would be delayed until December 26, that the package was in Orlando, FL. I asked the Lord if He would work that out for me. And He did! The box came just in time for Christmas.

I began to realize that there was anointing to overcome delays.

We have had many testimonies of delivery dates being moved up on items like furnace parts, cabinets, monies, and a pool after calling them in.

Here are two more testimonies to share.

I was to speak at a conference, and I forgot to order books. I ordered the books on July 28, with a delivery date of August 15, 10 days after my conference. I told the Lord I needed help on this, and I received the books on August 2—three days before I needed them!

Another time I ordered eyelash extensions on July 24 from Italy. I needed them by August 4 for the trip.

I received a tracking update August 3, they were "being inspected at the customs of Italy."

I said, "Lord, I wanted to take them with me."

I went to the mailbox on August 3, and there they were. I rushed back in and checked the tracking, and it said:

2022-08-03 12:59:00UTC

Delivered, In/At Mailbox, SAINT PETERSBURG, FL,33712

2022-08-03 02:21:55UTC

The shipment is being inspected at the customs of Italy

From Italy to my mailbox in Florida — on the same day!

What are eyelashes in the big scheme of thing? God is showing me He is breaking delays as part of His new move.

Are you experiencing a delay in an area?

As I said earlier, the anointing to end delays is transferable!

I release this anointing over your life, in the Name of Jesus.

Receive it and activate it by declaring the delay is over; call it forth.

"Before they even call out to me, I will answer them; before they've finished telling me what they need, I'll have already heard." —Isaiah 65:24 (NKJV)

DREAMING WITH GOD

I encounter many people who do not have a vision for life, much less the future. They are searching to find out what God wants them to do.

What they don't realize is that God has built a passion within us and a direction for life comes from that passion. Usually, the passion is something that stays at the forefront of our minds.

My dearest friend, Karen Elisabeth Williams, has a passion for teaching and child advocacy. Throughout her life, she has had the innate ability to see into a child's heart and know exactly what they need.

At one point, she had therapeutic daycare from her home, where the most marginalized children would be with her from 7 a.m.- 7 p.m. Monday through Friday. She would love them, help them find their value, and teach them in ways they could learn.

She didn't work with children her entire career. She had her own tree business, worked for a corporation, and at a church office. But the passion inside of her for children never left.

Karen Elisabeth started the children's program ten years ago at the Gathering Apostolic Center. Every child who attended has had the opportunity to encounter the love of Jesus, learn their identity in Him, and see the wonder of God displayed in their classroom.

Her future vision is to have a K-12 school for children to be equipped as world-changers for the Kingdom of God. She wants them to experience the love of Jesus and be equipped as high impact leaders in every sphere of influence.

Karen Elisabeth is partnering with God as the school's beginning stages are emerging! Her journey testifies to the passion that God built inside of her, which has directed her steps in her vision for the future.

UNCOVERING YOUR PASSION

Do you have a passion that keeps you motivated and moving forward no matter what obstacles you face?

It took me some time to discover and put into words my passion. From my passion came clarity and vision for the future.

In a nutshell, I am passionate about my family, health, oneness with God, and helping others know God and discover their destiny for the Kingdom. Everything I do now and for the future is filtered through these passions.

How do you discover your passion?

It is important to invite God into the process. He will bring things to mind that you never considered and stretch you to think outside your comfort zone.

Here are some of the steps to help you start brainstorming with God. Through this process, you will see a theme emerging for you to build your future vision.

The Word says, "For as he thinks in his heart, so is he." —Proverbs 23:7 (NKJV)

Once you can envision God's dream for you, a passion builds in you to bring the dream to life. That is when steps become clear on how to activate or bring your dream into reality.

The only way to achieve this is by partnering with God.

STEPS TO BUILD A YOUR VISION

1. Write down your passions

"Then the LORD answered me and said: 'Write the vision And make it plain on tablets, That he may run who reads it. For the vision is yet for

an appointed time; But at the end it will speak, and it will not lie. Though it tarries, wait for it; Because it will surely come, It will not tarry.'"
—Habakkuk 2:2-3 (NKJV)

My list started with God, my family, health, and finances. Next to each one, I wrote what I wanted, such as perfect health, being debt-free, family to find their calling, spouses, and travel. Slowly over the years, I would visualize, pray, and agree with God over my desires. I can do this because God says:

"Delight yourself also in the LORD, And He shall give you the desires of your heart." —Psalms 37:4 (NKJV)

"Beloved, I pray that you may prosper in all things and be in health, just as your soul prospers." —3 John 1:2 (NKJV)

I have seen many things come to fulfillment.

Here are a few.

- Debt-Free 2021, even after buying a new house in 2019

- Healed from an auto-immune disease

- Son married to Christian woman and stepping into full-time ministry

- Daughter opening a successful business

- Blessings of grandchildren and great-grandchildren, I have 8 grands and 2 greats so far.

There is something about partnering with God that opens new ways for blessings and favor to flow in your life.

2. Write down everything that you want to do, no matter how impossible it may seem.

Here are a few of mine. However, there are many more things I dream about that are desires of my heart.

- Write books that will transform lives
- Have a TV Program
- Create a Perfect Health Zone for Healing
- Travel the 7 Continents
- Building Apostolic Centers

Here is God's goodness to date:

- I have written five books
- I have created and launched a TV show
- God told me I have perfect health
- I have traveled to 5 of the 7 continents
- I have launched our first Apostolic Center

3. **Agreeing with God for the fulfillment of your dream** by declaring your vision, and trusting God to established it for you. (Job 22:28, paraphrased)

Begin to declare Scripture over your list. Scripture activates the move of Heaven on your behalf. When you agree with the Word of God, He is looking to act on the Word.

Then the LORD said to me, "You have seen well, for I am [actively] watching over My word to fulfill it." —Jeremiah 1:12 (AMP)

Here are a few of the Scriptures I used to declare over my list:

Family: "As for Me," says the LORD, "this is My covenant with them: My Spirit who is upon you, and My words which I have put in your mouth, shall not depart from your mouth, nor from the mouth of your descendants, nor from the mouth of your descendants' descendants," says the LORD, "from this time and forevermore." —Isaiah 59:21 (NKJV)

Finances: "And you shall remember the LORD your God, for it is He who gives you power to get wealth, that He may establish His covenant which He swore to your fathers, as it is this day." —Deuteronomy 8:18 (NKJV)

Health: "Beloved, I pray that you may prosper in all things and be in health, just as your soul prospers." —3 John 1:2 (NKJV)

Ministry: "But go rather to the lost sheep of the house of Israel. And as you go, preach, saying, 'The kingdom of heaven is at hand.' Heal the sick, cleanse the lepers, raise the dead, cast out demons. Freely you have received, freely give." —Matthew 10:6-8 (NKJV)

Go with Great Expectations

In closing, I want to send you knowing that these new moves of God are an invitation for you to join in. He is looking for your YES to follow Him into one of the most significant time in history.

You were born to live a long life with hope and a future! God is setting you up for His BEST! He will partner with you to expand the Kingdom. His blessings will overtake you as you accept His invitation.

Expect miracles!

In *The Message,* Amos 9:13-15 says:

"Yes indeed, it won't be long now." God's Decree. Things are going to happen so fast your head will swim, one thing fast on the heels of the other. You won't be able to keep up. Everything will be happening at once—and everywhere you look, blessings! Blessings like wine pouring off the mountains and hills..."

Go with Great Expectation and Abundant Blessing in all you do!

ABOUT CINDY STEWART

Cindy Stewart has an anointing to bring others into a deeper encounter with God by welcoming His presence and being obedient to the leading of the Holy Spirit. She ministers in the presence and power of the Lord. With her prophetic mantle, she discerns the heart of God for a generation that longs for a fresh and new connection to God. Most Sundays, you can find her preaching at The Gathering Apostolic Center.

Links for her books and TV show can be found at: Cindy-Stewart.com.